EVERYTHING I NEED TO KNOW
I LEARNED FROM

Betty White

100 YEARS OF WISDOM FROM
THE FIRST LADY OF TELEVISION

JULIANA SHARAF

Betty White
in 1975.

A Salute to the First Lady of Television

ONLY ONE NAME in television brings people together from all walks of life: Betty White. She's a showstopping tour de force with a natural talent for quick quips, sly comebacks and spreading joy wherever she goes. Betty's incredible story of working her way up from radio bit parts to producing and starring in her own television shows to ascending the ranks and arriving as small screen royalty is as much a testament to her work ethic as it is her boundless enthusiasm for making people feel good. Whether it's her iconic portrayals of beloved sitcom characters, her advocacy on behalf of animal welfare charities or her talent for penning powerful memoirs, it's clear the legendary Golden Girl still has untold tricks up her sleeve (because some folks just get better with time). No matter your age, Betty's got sage advice that will crack you up, make you smile and open your eyes to all the good things life has to offer.

Betty White voices Grammy Norma in *The Lorax* (2012). Among her other film and TV credits, the actress lent her voice to a tiger toy named Bitey White in *Toy Story 4* (2019).

Bea Arthur, Rue McClanahan and Betty White in *The Golden Girls*.

Talk It Out

Arguments happen. It's normal for things to occasionally get heated with the people we love. When that happens, it's best to settle your differences quickly and move on.

WHEN IT COMES to the staying power of *The Golden Girls*, part of the beloved hit show's charm centers on the rapid-fire exchanges between housemates Sofia Petrillo (Estelle Getty), Dorothy Zbornak (Bea Arthur), Blanche Devereaux (Rue McClanahan) and Rose Nylund (Betty White). By the season three episode "Three On a Couch," however, their bickering reaches a fever pitch, and the girls attempt to get a hold of their growing discord by attending a group therapy session. Seeking the advice of an impartial professional like Dr. Ashley

Talk It Out

(Philip Sterling) to foster communication and work toward a common solution certainly sounds like a healthy, positive experience—in theory. Instead, it's a no-holds-barred showdown that turns downright ugly as the women gang up on the eternally optimistic St. Olafian in their midst.

Despite her efforts to keep the peace, Rose finds herself on the receiving end of a barrage of biting insults. Blanche, always one to get an extra word in, takes it one step further, shamelessly castigating Rose for everything from her intelligence to her sense of style to her skills in the kitchen. When Dr. Ashley asks Rose to comment on this show of candid cruelty, a thoroughly stung Rose replies, "I think she's a *gerkonanaken*," which, as she explains, is "the precise moment when dog doo turns white," stunning Blanche into silence.

Eventually, after taking the time to air their grievances and let it all out, the four friends come to this simple but no less heartfelt conclusion: no matter how annoying they might find one another, nothing is worth ending one's cheesecake-based camaraderie.

Rue McClanahan as Blanche Devereaux and Betty White as Rose Nylund in *The Golden Girls*.

Betty White in a 1957 promotional photo for her show *Date With the Angels*.

It's OK to Change Your Mind

"The voice just wasn't that big. . . . Also, somewhere in there, I think I discovered boys and all kinds of other good stuff."

—BETTY WHITE

T MAY SOUND impossible after having watched her spend most of a lifetime onscreen, but Betty White's girlhood dream was to become an opera singer rather than a television trailblazer. As she told Rip Rense in 2017, "I was going for the dramatic soprano and coloratura. I could hit F above high C, and I was so proud," but admitting that, as a 14-year-old, she was probably a few years behind the curve in terms of training her vocal chords. In other words: "The only problem was it probably didn't sound very good." By switching gears and pursuing her love of writing, she wrote and performed in a school play. Before long, Betty caught the acting bug, and created a legacy that's lit up sets for generations. Don't be afraid to pursue a new calling. You never know where it might take you.

Betty White is all smiles in *The Proposal* (2009).

Nature Is Good for the Soul

When we explore our natural wonders, we gain a new appreciation of all the joys our land has to offer.

NOTHING SOOTHES THE soul like getting away from the hustle and bustle of our daily lives by heading deep into the wilderness. Far from the steel, concrete and glass palaces of cities or the manicured lawns of suburbia, we can wander for hours under wide open skies, cook our meals over a crackling fire and sleep sprawled out under the stars, joys Betty White learned at a young age thanks to her parents.

In her 2011 autobiography *If You Ask Me (And Of Course You Won't)*, the legendary actress called the childhood camping trips she

Nature Is Good for the Soul

spent exploring the High Sierras on horseback her "earliest, fondest memories." "In those days," she writes, "we would never see another human being during the whole three weeks—it was true wilderness. Heaven." Intrigued by the sight of the forest ranger hat her father donned on vacation, Betty wanted to become a forest ranger. But since women were not permitted in the role at the time, she resigned herself to admiring the wilderness as a humble camper.

Happily, her luck changed. Aware of Betty's deep-seated love of wilderness conservation, in 2010, the United States Forest Service made her an Honorary Forest Ranger at the Kennedy Center in Washington, D.C., presenting the actress with her very own forest ranger's hat. "He's been gone all these years, but...I would swear my dad was standing right there," she wrote of the ceremony, a touching tribute to the father who helped show her the beauty of America's great outdoors.

Take a note from Betty's book: Go outside and get some fresh air. It'll do you good in more ways than you can imagine.

A member of the U.S. Forest Service presents Betty with her honorary Forest Ranger award in Washington, D.C., on November 9, 2010.

Betty White
in 1986.

"Mind your own business, take care of your affairs and don't worry about other people so much."

—BETTY WHITE

Betty White shares a moment with Dr. Jane Goodall at the Third Annual Jane Goodall Global Leadership Awards in Beverly Hills, California, on October 30, 2009.

Do Your Part

Whether in times of war or peace, when we all come together and contribute our unique talents, insights and more—regardless of our age or individual skill sets—we can achieve great things.

THE MONTH BEFORE her 20th birthday, Betty's life and the lives of millions of Americans changed forever when Japanese forces attacked Pearl Harbor. Soon after, the United States declared war on the Axis Powers, and citizens of all stripes began to pitch in to help the war effort in whatever ways they could. For some, this meant shipping off to bring the fight to German and Japanese troops on foreign shores. But for many Americans, showing support for one's country entailed keeping busy on the home front, and for Betty, this meant putting her Hollywood hopes on hold and signing up for the American Women's Voluntary Services (AWVS).

Do Your Part

With as many as 325,000 volunteers at their peak, the uniformed women of the AWVS could be placed in any number of roles: selling war bonds, conducting aerial photography, delivering messages, working in emergency kitchens and more. Betty got things off to a roll literally by hopping behind the wheel as a Post Exchange (PX) truck driver, whose main task was to shuttle supplies up through the Hollywood Hills and make deliveries to soldiers' barracks.

The most entertaining part of her service by far, however, required a more personal touch. In the evenings, Betty and other members of the AWVS would attend rec halls and dance the night away with the troops due to ship out. In fact, these high-spirited soirées were where she met her first husband, a serviceman named Dick Barker.

As Betty told *Cleveland Magazine*, "It was a strange time and out of balance with everything." Nevertheless, their hard work and sacrifice paid off, and after the war, Betty and millions of others could get back to pursuing their dreams, all because they leaned in when their country needed them most. In times of difficulty, there's something to be said for pitching in as many ways as you can.

Betty White, c. 1954.

Betty White and Rue McClanahan in a scene from *The Golden Girls*.

First Impressions Aren't Everything

"I was wrong. You don't wear too much makeup."

—BETTY WHITE AS ROSE NYLUND

I T'S OFTEN SAID that first impressions are the most important. Despite our best intentions, though, the first time isn't always the charm, but it can still be pretty insightful, something Betty knows as Rose Nylund on *The Golden Girls*. When curiosity finally gets the better of Blanche Devereaux (Rue McClanahan) in the season three episode "Dorothy's New Friend," she asks Rose, "What was your first impression of me?" Smiling sweetly in her pastel sweater, Rose lays it all out on the table: "I thought you were a slut who wore too much makeup." But before Blanche can dwell on her brutal honesty, Rose breezily amends her previous statement while hurrying out the door. "I was wrong," she adds with a playful wave of her hand. "You don't wear too much makeup." It's not the end of the world if you don't make a good first impression. Just put your best foot forward and stay positive. Your real friends will see you as you are.

Betty White at home with her dogs Bandy, Stormy and Danny, c. 1954.

Laughter Lightens the Heart

Find the things that make you smile and laugh and hold on to them through the tough times.

BETTY CREDITS HER parents with three great gifts: her love of animals, her sense of humor and her optimism. Born to Horace and Tess White on January 17, 1922, Betty was just 7 years old when the stock market crashed and her parents started to feel the strain on the family finances. Rather than spiral into his own depression, Horace began making radios. And when strapped buyers couldn't pay up, Horace would trade his sets for dogs, which he then built kennels for at home.

Laughter Lightens the Heart

Despite wanting to help out neighbors or four-legged friends in need, Betty's parents faced a sad, deeply personal predicament. In a 1955 article in the *TV Radio Mirror*, Betty's mother Tess explained, " ...ever since she was a baby, we've had puppies for her to play with. We hoped they would help take the place of the brothers and sisters she couldn't have—because an auto accident took that possibility away from me shortly after her birth. It's for this reason we've always had dogs to help fill the house."

Thankfully, with a number of cuddly companions around, the White house was never a place filled with sadness or longing. Horace and Tess doted on their young daughter and enjoyed engaging her in their discussions at the dinner table. "My dad would always ask me how things were at school and somehow, we'd get into silliness and fun," she told *Momtastic.com* in 2012. "And we also would talk very seriously. It wasn't all giggle time. But, I think those [conversations] went a long way on teaching me how to appreciate the positives as opposed to the negatives."

Take it from Betty: Where there's laughter, there's a silver lining.

Be Yourself

"I just want to bring as much natural as I can."

—BETTY WHITE

ALTHOUGH NUMEROUS FAMOUS stars have flocked to study under the likes of Stella Adler, Lee Strasberg, Sanford Meisner and others to embrace the finer points of method acting, Betty never felt the need to engage in emotional recall or take part in acting workshops packed with other young hopefuls. Instead, she felt her own instincts were enough to guide her lines, preferring to stick to the old adage that acting is reacting. "I just want to bring as much natural as I can," she later confessed. "I'm not saying that people who take acting lessons are false. They're much better than I am, but it doesn't work for me." And her convictions certainly have not steered her wrong. When you know you've got a talent, sometimes the best thing you can do is listen to your gut. You might be onto something.

Writers Fran Van Hartesveldt, George Tibbles and Bill Kelsay join Betty on the set of *Date With the Angels* in 1957.

Betty poses with a snake at the Greater Los Angeles Zoo Association's 40th Annual "Beastly Ball" at the Los Angeles Zoo, June 19, 2010.

"Animal lover that I am, a cougar I am not."

—BETTY WHITE

Jane Leeves, Betty White, Valerie Bertinelli and Wendie Malick in a 2010 promotional photo for *Hot in Cleveland*.

It's All in the Attitude

There's a certain confidence that comes with having been around the block. But you don't have to wait until your golden years to accept yourself as you are.

BETTY WHITE'S MOST recent hit sitcom, TV Land's *Hot in Cleveland*, sees her as Elka Ostrovsky, a feisty adoptive matriarch to three 40-somethings from Los Angeles who decide to make Cleveland, Ohio, their new home after a chance emergency landing. As Melanie Moretti (Valerie Bertinelli), Joy Scroggs (Jane Leeves) and Victoria Chase (Wendie Malick) struggle with their various insecurities about relationships, careers and coming to terms with aging, Betty transcends the group as the one woman who's always sure of herself. Ironically, her blunt truths work like a scalpel, cutting through the self-doubts and other delusions plaguing the trio, and one such valuable teaching moment comes in the season four episode "Method Man."

Recently enrolled at a local college, Joy feels particularly out of touch while witnessing Elka, a fellow student, making waves as one of the popular "kids." When Joy asks Elka why she has an easier time socializing with the (considerably) younger crowd, Elka answers without batting an eye: "Because I'm 90. I'm a novelty. I'm also genuinely cool."

"And I'm their mum's age," Joy continues, visibly distressed. "No one wants their mum hanging out with them, or worse, acting like them."

In a blink-and-you'll-miss-it moment of pity, Elka simply adds, "You can't take it personally," five little words of wisdom that go a long way in terms of rolling with life's punches and playing the hand you've been dealt.

Like her Midwestern counterpart, Betty makes no effort to hide who she is, a trait that endears her to just about everyone. When you're honest with yourself, you allow others a chance to appreciate the real you.

Betty White as Elka Ostrovsky on *Hot in Cleveland.*

Betty White hosts *Saturday Night Live* on May 8, 2010.

Do What Scares You

"I have no regrets at all. None. I consider myself to be the luckiest old broad on two feet."

—BETTY WHITE

CONSIDERING SHE'S SPENT decades starring in sitcoms, game shows, movies and more, you'd be forgiven for thinking Betty White has done it all. But thanks to a viral Facebook petition making the internet rounds in February 2010, Lorne Michaels set out to fill one more role Betty hadn't taken: hosting *Saturday Night Live*. Despite her countless hours in front of the camera, the octogenarian television legend hesitated to accept, fearing she'd be "a fish out of water" alongside her considerably younger co-stars Bill Hader, Amy Poehler, Kristen Wiig and others (not to mention the use of cue cards, which she hates). But when the comic powerhouse took the famed stage at Studio 8H on May 8, she showed a whole new generation of fans she could still get big laughs live at 88 years old, all because she dared to show up and shine.

Betty White, Will Forte, Maya Rudolph and Ana Gasteyer appear in the *Saturday Night Live* cold-open sketch "The Lawrence Welk Show: Mother's Day," May 8, 2010. Welk's real-life variety show premiered in 1951, just two years before Betty starred in her first hit comedy, *Life With Elizabeth*.

Betty White greets the entertainment on the set of *The Betty White Show* in 1958.

Never Typecast Yourself

Throughout life, you may find people attempting to mold you to meet their expectations. That doesn't mean you have to conform. Hold your head high and keep doing your thing.

AFTER WORLD WAR II drew to a close and her work with the American Women's Voluntary Services (AWVS) came to an end, Betty White once again set her sights on making it in show business, pounding the pavement across the greater Los Angeles area in search of a job. Yet despite her moxie, talent and can-do attitude, Betty kept hearing the same frustrating refrain: that she was too "unphotogenic" to land the roles she craved. This troubling turn of events could've easily put the brakes on any aspiring actor's confidence. But rather than throw in the towel, Betty looked to her childhood for inspiration.

Never Typecast Yourself

Having booked her first radio gig at the tender age of 8, in which she voiced a crippled orphan on the show *Empire Builders*, Betty opted to give it another shot on the airwaves. Finally, a friendly producer by the name of Fran Van Hartesveldt decided he saw something special in Betty. His show: *The Great Gildersleeve*, a comedy sponsored by Kraft Foods, which at the time was angling to market its Parkay margarine product. Van Hartesveldt said, "I'll take a chance and give you one word to say in the commercial on this week's *Gildersleeve*...Think you can say 'Parkay' without lousing it up?" And just like that, Betty's fortunes started to turn. Although she later copped to being afraid she'd blurt out "parfait" instead, the young consummate professional nailed it. Before long, Betty began booking other bit parts on programs such as *Family Theater Radio* and *Blondie*, based on the comic strip by Chic Young.

You won't always measure up to other people's standards, and that's OK. Ignore the naysayers and stay focused on your goals. You'll get there.

"If one has no sense of humor,
one is in trouble."

—BETTY WHITE

Betty White
in 1999.

Say It With a Smile

**If someone starts patronizing you, feel free to
set the record straight (although you might want
to throw in a grin for good measure).**

NO ONE WANTS to be told how to do their job, especially
when you're an icon. Like Sue Ann Nivens, her fictional
counterpart on *The Mary Tyler Moore Show*, Betty knows
what it's like to work your way to the top of your field, to prove
yourself time and again. But when news anchor Ted Baxter (Ted
Knight) tries to tell Sue Ann how to read for the camera, it's just a
matter of time (read: seconds) before she puts him in his place.

Having carved a role for herself as the effervescent hostess of
the television cooking show *The Happy Homemaker*, Sue Ann has

made a living off dishing out helpful tips for housewives. But as soon as the cameras stop rolling, the backbiting maneater lurking beneath her saccharine shell comes out in full force. After keeping up the Jekyll and Hyde act for a few years, Sue Ann opts to switch gears by trying out for a newscaster role at her station in the season five episode "A Girl Like Mary."

Tasked with overseeing the news-reading audition for someone who could potentially become his next co-anchor, Ted brusquely explains, "Park it over here [the desk]. That's the camera. When the red light goes on, that means that the camera is about—"

"Ted," Sue Ann cuts in, her face stretched in her signature *Happy Homemaker* grin. "I know what I'm doing. Just cue me and stick a sock in it." Although it quickly becomes apparent Sue Ann's perky delivery doesn't quite gel with reading about a mudslide disaster, Ted hears her message loud and clear.

You deserve to be treated with respect. Don't be afraid to remind people of that.

Betty as Sue Ann Nivens in a 1974 publicity portrait for *The Mary Tyler Moore Show.*

Tell It Like It Is

"Do you think it's easy to be cheerful around you two?"

—BETTY WHITE AS ROSE NYLUND

EVERYONE HAS A limit, and Betty's no exception as Rose Nylund in *The Golden Girls*. In the season one episode "The Flu," the friends find themselves stuck at home under the weather and quickly take to getting on each other's last nerve. Fed up with Rose's attempts to take everyone's minds off their symptoms, Dorothy makes no effort to hide her ever-mounting frustrations, yelling, "I've had it up to here with your cheerful disposition!" But Rose, floored at Dorothy's dig, doesn't back down. The gloves are off as she tells Dorothy and Blanche, "Do you think it's easy to be cheerful around you two? Do you know how many of these stinking hot toddies I have to drink to keep on a happy face?" When you've been pushed past your breaking point, sometimes it's best to speak up and make yourself heard.

Betty meets the L.A. Angels as Vickie Angel in *Date With the Angels*, 1957. One of the show's writers, Fran Van Hartesveldt, helped Betty land a gig on the radio program *The Great Gildersleeve*.

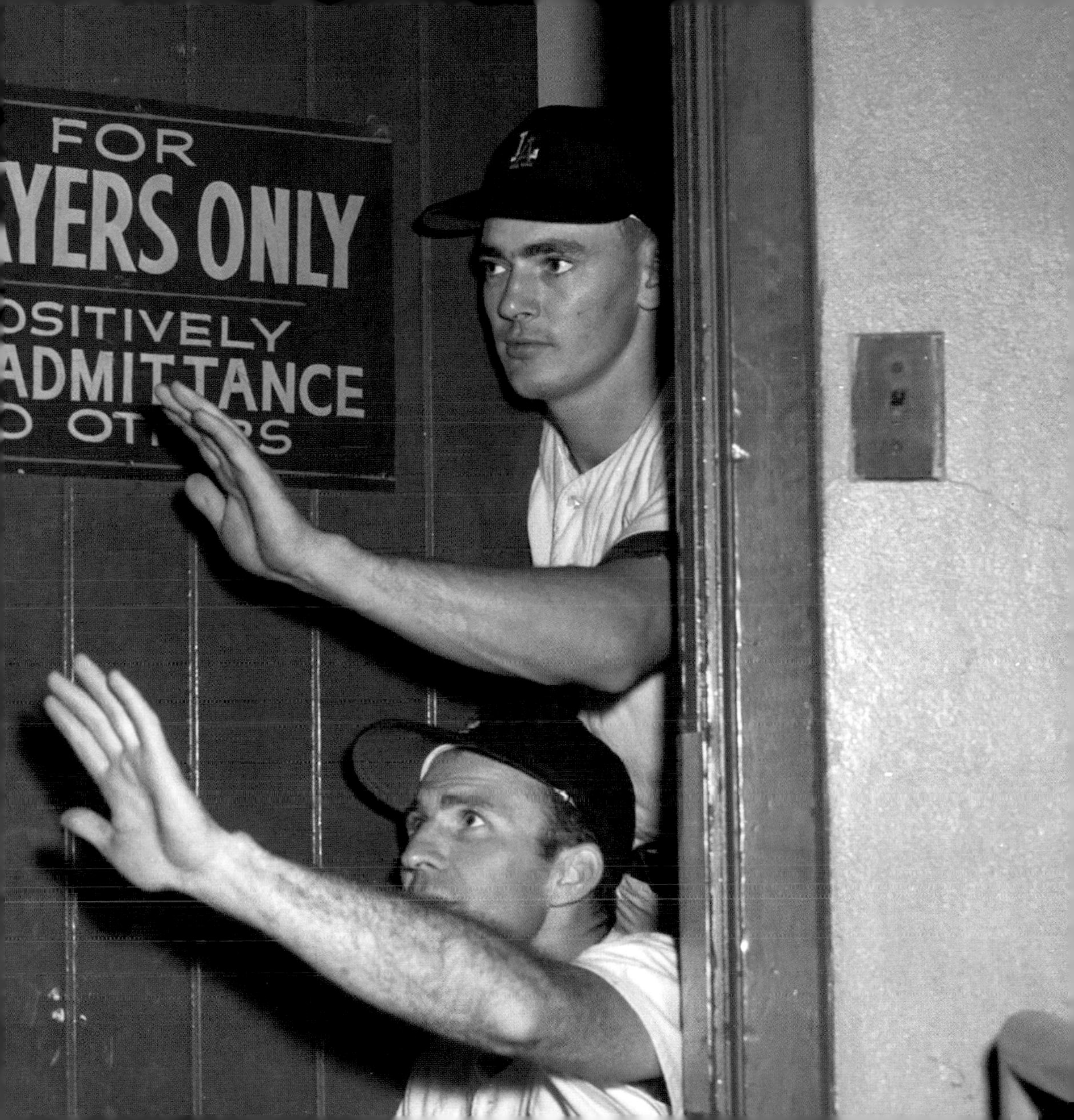
FOR
YERS ONLY
OSITIVELY
ADMITTANCE

KLAC·TV

Betty White (left) and Eddie Albert stand in front of the camera during a broadcast of *Hollywood on Television* in 1952.

Make It Up As You Go

Very few careers have linear paths, and that can be a good thing. You never know what opportunities will lead to your big break.

DESPITE DOING BIT parts and later moving on to leads on local radio shows, a 20-something Betty still yearned to step out from behind the microphone and step in front of the camera. After a local DJ asked her to sing on his variety program, the tenacious young actress landed a gig answering phones on a panel show called *Grab Your Phone*. In fact, she was so charming while chatting up guests, management pulled her aside to say, in her words, "Don't tell the other girls [manning the phones] because they're only getting $5 but [because] you can ad-lib with

Make It Up As You Go

the MC, you get $10." And while *Grab Your Phone* only ran for a year, it was more than enough time for Betty to grab the attention of Los Angeles DJ Al Jarvis, who asked her to join his new televised talk show, *Hollywood on Television.*

Airing for six days a week, *Hollywood on Television* required Betty to ad-lib alongside Al for a grueling five-and-a-half hours a day—all in front of a live audience. As Betty told NPR in 2014, "Whatever happened, you had to handle it. There was never any rehearsal or script or anything. Whoever came in that door was on, and you were interviewing them." With so many hours to fill, the entertainment portion of the program quickly evolved to include comedy sketches. When asked if she could stretch one about a husband and wife into a half-hour, Betty said, "'It won't work . . . the jokes won't hold up that long, you can't do a half-hour.' That's how much I knew," she added with a laugh. But she pulled it off, and the resulting product became the basis of her 1951 hit show, *Life With Elizabeth.*

The lesson: You don't have to know the next step. Just shine where you are and keep moving forward. You'll find a way.

Betty White and Lucille Ball at the release of Betty's memoir *Betty White in Person* in 1987.

Seek Out a Mentor

**Find someone who not only understands
your goals and aspirations but can help guide
you when the going gets tough.**

AS SOMEONE WHO predates sliced bread by six years,
Betty White's got a veritable mountain of television and
film credits to her name. As a rare female producer in the
1950s, however, Betty had a lot to prove in an industry dominated by
male studio executives. Fortunately, she had a fellow trailblazer and
kindred spirit by her side.

Just two years before Betty cofounded Bandy Productions (named
for her Pekingese, Bandit) in 1952, another television legend
formed her own production company. Named Desilu Productions
to accommodate her name as well as her husband's, Lucille Ball

launched the company to produce her hit CBS sitcom, *I Love Lucy*. Aside from managing her show, however, Lucy's handling of the business's creative side included green lighting the production of other programs such as *Star Trek*, *The Untouchables*, *Mission: Impossible* and more. After meeting on the Culver Studios lot, the two became fast friends, united by their colorful personalities, love of hard work and keen senses of humor.

Despite being 11 years her senior, Lucy leaned on Betty for support during her divorce from Desi Arnaz in 1960. Years later, she repaid the favor when Betty lost her husband, Allen Ludden, to cancer in 1981. As Betty told Reddit in a 2014 AMA forum, "Lucy was one of my dearest friends. . . . She was dynamite. Everything you saw was what you got. We used to play backgammon, and she used to teach me the game but she used to move the pieces so fast. I used to say, 'How are you teaching me if you move the pieces so fast?' and she would say, 'I want to win!'"

When you come across someone with experience who inspires you to achieve your dreams, don't just think of them as an ally. They could become a friend for life.

Betty gets all dolled up as part of a fashion shoot for The Lifeline Program in Culver City, California, May 9, 2012.

"I had my eyes done in 1976 and have let nature take its course ever since. As for my hair, I have no idea what color it really is, and I never intend to find out."

—BETTY WHITE

Betty White gets cheeky with Gerard Butler on *The Tonight Show with Jay Leno* on January 12, 2012.

Don't Let Age Get in the Way

"My answer to anything under the sun, like 'What have you not done in the business that you've always wanted to do?' is 'Robert Redford.'"

—BETTY WHITE

ONE NAME INEVITABLY pops up in nearly all of Betty's interviews: Robert Redford. Having fallen for him after watching his performance in *Out of Africa* (1985), the smitten Queen of Television has since delighted in namedropping her cinema crush. Redford, for his part, relishes her affection and once sent her a whopping six-stanza poem (which, unfortunately for the rest of us, she has chosen to keep to herself). Beyond Redford, Betty's lighter flirtations include George Clooney and Gerard Butler, the latter of whom she asked on *The Tonight Show with Jay Leno*, "How do you feel about older women?" If Betty's feisty spirit is any indication, age has no bearing on your ability to turn up the heat. It's never too late to put something you want out into the universe.

Love Animals

Our feathery, furry and scaly friends have a lot to teach us about compassion, kindness and looking out for the planet we share.

ONG BEFORE SHE began studying opera or pining to become a forest ranger, Betty spent her earliest years dreaming of being a zookeeper, a passion she claims was passed on to her by her parents, self-described zoophiles Horace and Tess White. In her 2011 book *Betty & Friends: My Life at the Zoo*, she writes, "My interest started early on, tagging after my mom and dad, who went to the zoo often, not just to please their little girl but because they enjoyed the experience. . . . My folks also taught me to discriminate between the 'good zoos' and those other

Betty cuddles with a chimpanzee in 1974.

places that displayed animals for all the wrong reasons and sent you home feeling sad." These fun-filled educational outings left a lasting impression on Betty, who has devoted much of her off-screen life to championing animal conservation efforts by groups such as the Morris Animal Foundation, the Los Angeles Zoo Commission, the African Wildlife Foundation, Actors & Others for Animals and many more. She even managed to combine her two greatest passions by producing and hosting *The Pet Set*, a 1971 television show in which the icon interviewed celebrities like James Stewart, Carol Burnett, Burt Reynolds and others about their adorable animal companions.

Beyond hosting charity events or enjoying one-on-one visits with Koko, the legendary gorilla who communicated through sign language, Betty's always been one to make sure her love of animals begins at home. Regardless of her hectic schedule, the nonagenarian has long made a point of caring for furry companions over the years, which she calls "first-rate therapists." As she explains it, "You know that when they tell you something, they mean it. They just love you, it's that simple." Take it from Betty: Animals can add a great deal of joy to your life without saying a word.

Betty White meets James Brolin and his harlequin Great Dane, Buck, on *The Pet Set* in 1971.

Rose (Betty) reunites
with her biological father,
Brother Martin (Don Ameche),
a monk from St. Olaf on
The Golden Girls.

There's No Place Like Home

"Back in St. Olaf..."

—BETTY WHITE AS ROSE NYLUND

EVEN IF YOU left the place where you grew up in search of greener pastures, you carry a bit of that community with you wherever you go. For Rose (Betty) on *The Golden Girls*, that means regaling Blanche, Dorothy and Sophia with larger-than-life tales of St. Olaf, Minnesota, and its quirky Norwegian inhabitants. Whether it's reminiscing about the time she lost the Butter Queen pageant due to "churn tampering," the year Nazis invaded the town, the annual Festival of the Dancing Sturgeons (in which everyone gathers to watch fish flop around on a deck) or the stark beauty of the "giant black hole" in front of the town courthouse, Rose is brimming with stories only St. Olafians can truly appreciate. Remember to take pride in your past, no matter how far you roam.

Betty and a furry friend in a promotional photo for *Date With the Angels*.

Follow Your Moral Compass

Find out what you value and let it be your guide. Don't be afraid to go against the grain if it means sticking up for what you know is right.

DESPITE HER WELL-KNOWN reputation as a workaholic, Betty White is no stranger to turning down projects when she objects to their content. As any veteran actor knows, saying "no" to roles can be tricky, especially if you remember what it's like to struggle to find work in Hollywood. Nonetheless, the only thing Betty loves more than acting is animals, a lifelong passion that made it relatively easy for her to decline a part in *As Good As It Gets* (1997).

The film stars Jack Nicholson as Melvin Udall, a misanthropic author living with severe obsessive–compulsive disorder. Annoyed by the sounds of his neighbor's escaped dog and overwhelmed by the interruption in his writing routine, Melvin hurls the helpless canine down a laundry chute, a heartless move for which he is later berated. Although the friendly pup ultimately emerges frightened but otherwise unscathed, after learning of the scene, Betty was clear with director James L. Brooks: She wanted no part of the picture.

"I know it's for laughs," she explains in *If You Ask Me (And Of Course You Won't)*, "but given my feelings about animals and my work for animal welfare, I just didn't find it funny." Well aware of her responsibility as a figure in the public eye, she added, "I didn't think it would be a good example to people who might try it in real life." And whenever the question of whether or not she regrets turning down the role pops up, Betty's answer has always been an unequivocal "No."

When something conflicts with what you know is true, fair or good, remember: It's up to you to do what you know is correct.

Betty White cuddles
a pair of Labrador
Retrievers in 1986.

Betty and her Pekingese, Bandit, relaxing at home, c. 1950s.

*"Animals don't lie.
Animals don't criticize.
If animals have moody days,
they handle them better
than humans do."*

—BETTY WHITE

Allen Ludden
and Betty White
on their wedding
day at the Sands
Hotel in Las Vegas,
June 14, 1963.

It's the Little Things

**Grand romantic gestures are all well and good.
But it's the small personal touches
that can really make someone feel special.**

I N 1961, A 39-year-old Betty White had already made a good deal of headway in her Hollywood career. With sitcoms like *Life With Elizabeth* and *Date With the Angels* under her belt, Betty started eyeing game shows and took a role as a celebrity guest on the popular CBS program *Password*, where she quickly found herself smitten with the show's host.

A widower with three children, Allen Ludden had warmth, wit, humor and thoughtfulness in spades, qualities he likewise saw in his newest guest panelist. But as a twice-divorced and happily single

It's the Little Things

woman of 10 years, Betty hesitated when he asked her to marry him, especially since their professional commitments had them working on opposite coasts. She put the matter off for a whole year, during which time Allen even took to wearing her engagement ring on a chain around his neck. Finally, when Easter came along, he tried a different approach. Sensing her hesitation stemmed from fear rather than doubt, Allen sent Betty a stuffed white bunny with a pair of diamond earrings clipped to its ears and a note that read, "Please say YES." Animal lover that she is, Betty was delighted by the gesture, and the happy couple wed in 1963.

But as Betty knows, the most memorable tokens of affection are beautifully simple. "Jewelry is lovely…but I think a handwritten letter—a lot of guys don't realize what that means," she told the *Sydney Morning Herald* in 2011. "All through our marriage, I opened something and there'd be a little note from Allen: 'Have I told you lately I loved you?'" Her doting husband knew this lesson well: You can't put a price on true romance. Sometimes it's the little romantic touches that say the most.

Betty and Allen
Ludden in 1972.

Stay Humble

"I got an award for everything. Inhaling, exhaling . . .
I've been so spoiled rotten."

—BETTY WHITE

YOU MIGHT THINK winning a Los Angeles Emmy Award at just 30 would've tempted Betty to let the fame go to her head. And while her incredible list of awards and accomplishments include eight Emmy Awards, a Grammy, three Screen Actors Guild Awards (including a Lifetime Achievement Award) and even a Daytime Emmy for her role as host of the game show *Just Men!*, Betty's never been one to brag about her accolades. Instead, the television icon chooses to focus on her fans, or as she explains in *If You Ask Me (And Of Course You Won't)*, people who "have been inviting me into their homes for decades." "When you walk into some place and a perfect stranger is your friend," she told *Entertainment Tonight*, "that's a great privilege." As Betty knows, it's best to let your work speak for itself.

Betty White celebrates her win at the 48th Annual Emmy Awards in Pasadena, California, September 8, 1996.

Bill Williams, John Gaunt, Leonard Goldenson and Betty White at a press showing of *Date With the Angels*, May 1, 1957. Williams was best known for starring in the Western television show *The Adventures of Kit Carson*, which aired from 1951 to 1955.

Life Isn't Always Fair

**Even when things don't work out in your favor,
be the bigger person and take the high road.**

KNOWING WHEN TO let things go is a crucial part of growing up. But there are some things you just don't have it in you to part from, as Rose (Betty) realizes on *The Golden Girls*' season three episode "Old Friends." After accidentally giving away Rose's favorite stuffed animal, a teddy bear affectionately named Fernando, Blanche attempts to explain the situation to its new owner, a bratty young neighborhood girl named Daisy (Jenny Lewis). Daisy is willing to part with the bear... for a price. Determined to get what her parents won't buy her, the scheming Sunshine Cadet (a sort

Life Isn't Always Fair

of Girl Scout) demands a 10-speed Schwinn bike in exchange for Fernando. When Blanche desperately insists the whole thing was a terrible mistake, Daisy holds the bear for ransom and ups the price, even cutting off one of its ears and sending it to the house to show she means business. Rose, naturally, is beside herself after finding out what has become of her bear, urging Blanche to make things right.

Eventually, Daisy comes back with Fernando in tow, apologizing for her past actions, only to renegotiate the deal—this time, she wants cash instead. But when Blanche offers to pay up, Rose steps in, telling Daisy, "If after all the years of love and companionship Fernando and I are meant to part company, I'll just have to accept that. Time to time, life deals you an unfriendly hand. There's nothing you can do about it. I guess there's a lesson to be learned here," she says, walking Daisy to the front door. "Sometimes life just isn't fair, kiddo." Just when it looks like she's given up Fernando for good, Rose grabs her beloved bear and tosses Daisy out of the house, slamming the door behind her. No, you can't always get what you want—and sometimes, that's for the best.

Betty White and Ed Asner on *The Mary Tyler Moore Show.*

Agree to Disagree

"I know just what you mean, Lou."

—BETTY WHITE AS SUE ANN NIVENS

AS THE lust-fueled maneater Sue Ann Nivens on *The Mary Tyler Moore Show*, Betty shows her colleague Lou Grant (Ed Asner) what it means to lend a sympathetic ear when he voices his concerns about their friend Mary Richards's (Mary Tyler Moore) newest boyfriend, Joe Warner (Ted Bessell)—namely, his penchant for public displays of affection. Due to his paternal instincts, Lou is wary of Mary's latest beau and tells Sue Ann, "A guy doesn't have to be all hands." "I know just what you mean, Lou," Sue Ann says, reminiscing about her own amorous encounters. "I couldn't agree less, but I know just what you mean." After all, you don't have to see eye-to-eye with someone to understand where they're coming from.

Betty White and Jack Carson (right) on the set of *The Betty White Show* in 1958.

"Butterflies are like women—we may look pretty and delicate, but baby, we can fly through a hurricane."

—BETTY WHITE

Betty White,
c. 1954.

The Show Must Go On

**Setbacks are bound to happen.
Don't let that stop you from achieving your goals.**

BY THE early 1950s, Betty White had not only made the leap from radio to television but worked her way up to a co-hosting gig on the show *Hollywood on Television,* which paved the way for her award-winning program *Life With Elizabeth.* But this newfound success did not come without its drawbacks. In addition to the physical exhaustion wrought from months of filming for hours on end before live audiences, Betty dealt with her own share of emotional setbacks from two divorces. Her first marriage, to Dick Barker, lasted only six months after he spirited her away from sunny L.A. to live on an Ohio chicken farm. Two years later, after marrying Hollywood agent Lane Allen in 1947, Betty thought she'd finally found the right person to settle down with. Lane's notion of settling down, however, meant asking Betty to give up her dream of working in show business to become a homemaker. Dismayed and heartbroken, Betty refused to bend; following the divorce, she moved back in with her parents.

Putting her failed romances firmly in the rearview mirror, the determined young actress threw herself mind, body and spirit into her career. But just as things couldn't look any more hopeful, the night before Betty was to film the first nationally televised episode of *Life With Elizabeth*, one of her dogs, a prized Pekingese, died after a sudden illness. It was a devastating loss. As Betty's mother, Tess, explained to *TV Radio Mirror* in 1954, "She cried all night." Rather than let the pressure break her, in a moment of clarity, Betty remembered she still had a job to do and a show only she could pull off. The next day, she wiped her tears and went to work "hoping she could bring happiness into someone else's life," her mother said.

No one is immune to heartbreak. In those low moments, focus on how far you've come and have faith things will work out.

Bandit (a.k.a. "Bandy") the Pekingese cuddles with Betty at home in 1954.

Betty White with actress Amanda Blake at a Benefit for Animals event.

Always Be Kind

"Cocktail party small talk may not be much worth hearing, but it's tough when you can't hear it at all."

—BETTY WHITE

YOU NEVER know what someone else might be going through. In her younger days, the icon got a firsthand look at the hardships of getting older by noticing how her father, Horace, started becoming more solitary at parties and social gatherings. He claimed he could never hear anyone in a crowd, but the truth was harder to swallow: Horace was losing his hearing. "I can remember accusing my dad of selective hearing," or hearing only what he wanted to hear, she writes in *If You Ask Me (And Of Course You Won't)*. "Shame on me. That was before I learned how isolated one can feel when [he] misses a key remark and loses track of the conversation but is loath to admit it." Remember: Not every disability or circumstantial condition is visible. Be compassionate.

Betty White (right) guest stars with Carol Burnett in a sketch from *The Carol Burnett Show*, May 28, 1977. Betty, along with Rue McClanahan, would later join the cast of *Mama's Family*, a spin-off based on a sketch from Burnett's show.

No Friends Like Old Friends

Make time to connect with the people who've stuck by your side through thick and thin.

WHEN YOU'VE been around as long as Betty has, you can expect to be on a first-name basis with more than a few industry insiders. Along with Lucille Ball, one of Betty's longest-running friendships was with the late comic actor, writer and director Carl Reiner, whom she got to know through her husband, Allen Ludden.

While serving in World War II, Carl met Capt. Allen Ludden during an audition for a spot in the Army Entertainment section, a performance group designed to boost morale with musical and

QUIZ KIDS

TREASURE
HUNT

WHO
DO YOU
TRUST?

$64,0

HOLLYWOOD
SQUARES

COLLEGE
BO

JEOP

DON

YOU BET
YOUR LIFE

TRUTH
OR
CONSEQUENCES

LIAR'S CLUB

Ralph Edwards, Carl Reiner,
Betty White and George
Fenneman in a press photo
for *Those Wonderful TV
Game Shows* (1984).

theatrical offerings. Impressed by Carl's impressions of Jimmy Stewart, Charles Boyer and Akim Tamiroff, Allen recruited him into the troupe, and the two became good friends. Almost 20 years later, when the *Password* host introduced Carl to his new bride, Betty, Carl was thrilled. "I consider her my captain-in-law," Carl later said. Through his work creating, producing, writing and acting on *The Dick Van Dyke Show*, Carl helped launch the career of Mary Tyler Moore, setting the stage for Betty's eventual Emmy-winning run as Sue Ann Nivens on *The Mary Tyler Moore Show*.

Betty and Carl stayed close after her husband's passing, and when Betty took on the role of Elka Ostrovsky on TV Land's *Hot in Cleveland*, Carl guest starred as Elka's boyfriend, Max Miller. In between filming, the comedy legend would sometimes ask Betty, "Wouldn't Allen get a kick out of this if he were here—seeing us working together?" The two later worked on a 2017 episode of the Freeform sitcom *Young & Hungry* and remained cherished friends right up until Carl's passing in 2020, a poignant reminder that old friendships really can change your life so long as you keep looking out for each other.

Betty White and Carl Reiner play long-lost lovers in a 2017 episode of *Young & Hungry*.

Stand Up for Others

"You don't buzz a legend!"

—BETTY WHITE

OVER THE COURSE of their careers, enterprising women like Lucille Ball and Betty White banded together to weather life's storms. Their sisterly bond can be seen in a 1988 episode of the game show *Super Password*, one of Lucy's final television appearances. Having recently suffered a stroke, the titian-haired trailblazer struggled to come up with a single clue for the password "Stiff." When Lucy's time ran out, despite being on the opposing team, Betty took host Bert Convy to task, saying, "You don't buzz a legend!" Although the audience roared with laughter, Betty's stone cold glare said it all: If you mess with Lucy, you'll be dealing with me. Fight for others, particularly when things aren't going their way. You never know when you'll need someone in your corner.

Betty White,
c. 1956.

Betty and Mary Tyler Moore attend the Annual Meeting of the Morris Animal Foundation in Los Angeles, June 22, 1985.

"Friendship takes time
and energy if it's going to work.
You can luck into something
great, but it doesn't last
if you don't give it
proper appreciation."

—BETTY WHITE

Brett Somers, Charles Nelson Reilly, Richard Dawson, Gene Rayburn and Betty White on *Match Game*, c. 1973.

BRETT

...ARLES

DOLLY

RICHARD

BETT...

Seek Joy

Carve out a few moments every day to do something you love.

STEPPING ONTO THE set of *Password* didn't just help Betty meet the love of her life—it provided her with a way to keep her spirits up during a quiet period in her career. Dedicated fans of a certain age may recall that following the end of *The Betty White Show*, Betty appeared on variety and talk shows, but always as a guest rather than a host.

Frustrated and disheartened by blistering reviews written by critics like the famously caustic John Crosby (who took no shame in mocking Betty about everything from her dimples to her voice to her wholesome image), the actress sought comfort by performing in summer stock productions in 1962 alongside her soon-to-be-

Seek Joy

husband, Allen Ludden. Emboldened in part by the warm welcome she received on *Password* after returning from their honeymoon, Betty soon made her way around the game show circuit, appearing on *Match Game, What's My Line, The Hollywood Squares, Your First Impression* and more. Dazzling viewers with her charm, wit and high spirits, she had a knack for outshining the competition and soon earned the moniker "the First Lady of Game Shows."

Years later, following her success on *The Mary Tyler Moore Show, The Carol Burnett Show* and a third iteration of *The Betty White Show* (this time a sitcom), in 1983, Betty finally got her turn running a game show in the form of *Just Men!* She knocked it out of the park, becoming the first woman to win a Daytime Emmy Award for Outstanding Game Show Host—and it all started because at one point in her career, she had chosen to have a bit of fun.

Make time for the things that make you smile. Even if everything else isn't going your way, the joy you create will keep you going until things work out. Who knows—your hobbies might be the spark for a whole new phase of your life.

Keep It Real

"Bets . . . you can't sidestep the truth."

—BETTY'S MOTHER, TESS WHITE

NO MATTER WHERE life takes us, there's no escaping the fact that we must all live with the choices we make. It's a guiding principle Tess White instilled in her daughter long before Betty White set foot on a television set, one Betty shares in *If You Ask Me (And Of Course You Won't)*. As Tess used to say, "Bets, you can lie to anyone in the world and even get away with it, perhaps, but when you are alone and look into your own eyes in the mirror, you can't sidestep the truth. Always be sure you can meet those eyes directly." It's easy to get caught up in fame and success, especially when that involves becoming a Hollywood legend. Keep your ego in check and be accountable for your actions.

WJM-TV
NEWS

Ed Asner, Betty White and Gavin MacLeod in a scene from *The Mary Tyler Moore Show*. Betty took home the Emmy Award for Outstanding Supporting Actress in a Comedy Series for her portrayal of Sue Ann Nivens in 1975 and 1976.

Bill Williams and Betty White in a publicity photo for *Date With the Angels*, c. 1957.

Honor Your Commitments

**When you give your word, plan on keeping
it to the best of your ability.**

EVERY SEASONED THESPIAN has their share of on-set horror stories. Whether it's a conflict of intention with a director, a lack of chemistry with a scene partner or a miscommunication with the costume department about what "size 6" really means, the drama created by making a work of fiction can have real-life consequences. For Betty White, only one project has ever made her want to jump ship: the short-lived ABC sitcom *Date With the Angels*, which ran from 1957 to 1958.

Sponsored by Chrysler, the show starred Betty and Bill Williams as Vicki and Gus Angel, a newlywed couple prone to flights of fancy and getting themselves into comedic shenanigans. Loosely based on the Elmer Rice play *Dream Girl*, the show featured long fantasy sequences written around Vicki's propensity for over-the-top daydreams. Given its female lead's knack for timing and previous experience on *Life With Elizabeth*, *Date With the Angels* had all the makings of a surefire hit. Unfortunately for everyone involved, Chrysler executives still weren't sold on the show's unconventional angle and ultimately nixed the dream sequences in favor of traditional at-home scenes. Its creative heart ripped out, the show was set adrift in a sea of sub-par ratings, and there was little Betty could do beyond watching it sink.

When the axe mercifully came down on *Angels* after just 33 episodes, Betty knew she still had 13 weeks of airtime to fill per her contract. Knowing no script rewrite could save the doomed show nor sway its shortsighted sponsors, rather than sulk at the loss, she boldly tossed the whole format by rebooting her variety program, *The Betty White Show*, to finish out the season strong.

We can't always control what happens to us, but we can always choose to make the most of the way we approach the commitments we've made. That starts with committing to having a good attitude.

Betty gets a final touch up before filming an episode of *Date With the Angels*, c. 1957.

"Be grateful for whatever praise you receive, but take it with a grain of salt."

—BETTY WHITE

Take the Note

Keep yourself open to receiving constructive criticism.
It might pay off better than you ever hoped.

I N THE THEATER world, "take the note" is a polite but firm way of telling an actor their approach isn't working and they should go in a different direction (usually said after a bit of pushback). Every actor knows it well, including Betty. As far as her iconic run on *The Golden Girls* is concerned, it's practically inconceivable to imagine a Rose by any other name. But that might've been the case had she insisted on playing the part of Blanche rather than listening to pilot director Jay Sandrich.

Knowing Betty and Rue McClanahan had co-starred on the

Rue McClanahan and
Betty White, c. 1988.

recently canceled NBC sitcom *Mama's Family* and were not likely to be available for long, Sandrich promptly invited them to audition for the show early in the casting process. Considering Betty's run as the lascivious Sue Ann Nivens on *The Mary Tyler Moore Show* and Rue's role as the sweet but dim Vivian Harmon on *Maude* (Bea Arthur's hit sitcom), producers thought it made sense to have Rue read for Rose and for Betty to audition as Blanche. But as the icon told *The Associated Press* in 2010, Sandrich said, "If Betty plays another nymphomaniac they are going to think it is Sue Ann Nivens all over again. . . . Why don't we switch them?'"

Intrigued by the challenge of portraying an innocent character without a hint of sarcasm, Betty nailed the part, while Rue was delighted to bring her unique brand of Southern charm to the part of Blanche. This critical swap persuaded Bea Arthur to take the role of Dorothy Zbornak, and the rest is television history.

It's normal to want to defend your work or go with what you do best, but in doing so, you might miss the forest for the trees. A fresh perspective can point you in a different, possibly better, direction.

Rue McClanahan,
Bea Arthur,
Estelle Getty and
Betty White as
The Golden Girls.

Del Moore and Betty White in a scene from *Life With Elizabeth.*

Do the Right Thing

We can't always count on others to do right by everyone. But where others fail, we can put our foot down and take a stand.

I N 1954, JUST two years after receiving her Los Angeles Emmy Award for Outstanding Personality for her work on *Life With Elizabeth*, Betty White produced and hosted her own television program, *The Betty White Show*, on NBC. Finding herself in the highly enviable position of exerting creative control over her own daytime variety show, the 32-year-old boldly hired a female director and looked to showcase the best talent around, no matter the color of their skin.

Today, a shrinking number of viewers can recall the dark days when audiences were segregated and not all performers were welcomed at hot ticket venues due to their race. Regardless of the Jim Crow attitudes of that time, Betty saw no reason not to book Arthur Duncan, a talented up-and-coming tap dancer, to grace her stage and show the folks at home a thing or two about fancy footwork. Yet as televisions in the deep South lit up with the image of Duncan proudly showing off his skills, racist studio execs balked at giving Betty's show airtime because Duncan was black.

Faced with angry pro-segregationists seeking to boycott her program, Betty had a choice: pull Duncan from her roster or get pulled from the lineup. Brassy as ever, her message was clear: "I'm sorry," she said. "Live with it." Betty stood by Duncan, and her show was canceled. But nothing can keep a good woman down, and the television tour de force later landed a starring role on the ABC sitcom *Date With the Angels*. Decades later, it's still a poignant reminder that each of us has the power to stand by our convictions, even when public opinion says otherwise.

Estelle Getty, Rue McClanahan, Betty White and Bea Arthur in *The Golden Girls*. In 1988, the cast performed live at the Royal Variety Performance in London at the invitation of Queen Elizabeth II.

Betty at the Museum of Radio and TV in Los Angeles, California, March 29, 2011.

Have a Hobby

**Live life to the fullest by getting involved with activities
and causes that go beyond your day job.**

AS ONE OF HOLLYWOOD'S most famous workaholics,
Betty's career has stretched on for a whopping 70 years
and counting. But just because she's known as the First
Lady of Television doesn't mean Betty's limited her sizable list of
accomplishments to the small screen. Always one to keep busy, the
golden girl has embarked on some remarkable side projects over the
years, making the most of her time off set in surprising ways.

Driven by her love of supporting animal welfare, Betty made a
splash in 2010 by branching into the clothing industry, lending

Have a Hobby

her likeness to a line of T-shirts and sweatshirts by Jerry Leigh, a Los-Angeles based clothing company. Naturally, a portion of the proceeds benefited the Morris Animal Foundation, an animal health charity that has been near and dear to her heart for decades (especially since she's a trustee).

A voracious reader, Betty first decided to try her hand at writing in 1983 by penning *Betty White's Pet-Love: How Pets Take Care of Us*. *Betty & Friends: My Life at the Zoo*, published in 2011, marked her seventh title to date, two of which she also recorded as audiobooks. To her delight, in February 2012, Betty won a Grammy award for her recording of *If You Ask Me (And Of Course You Won't)*—at the age of 90, no less—a fact made all the more exceptional because she has not once put her acting career on hold.

At home, the television legend fills what little remains of her downtime exercising her mental faculties by playing poker and doing crossword puzzles (her friend Tom Sullivan told CNN her puzzle books number in the "thousands"). If a star like Betty can make time for the things that bring her joy, you can and should, too.

Betty White
in 2009.

"Laughter keeps everyone feeling wonderful."

—BETTY WHITE

Never Take Yourself Too Seriously

"That's not what your girlfriend says."

—BETTY WHITE

DURING SUPER BOWL XLIV, Betty White elevated the Super Bowl ad to an art form. Starring in a Snickers commercial, the icon takes to the field as one of the guys in a game of tackle football. From the first play, it's clear she can't hold her own and is soon laid flat on her back in the mud. "Mike! What is your deal, man?" a teammate asks. Another chimes in, "You're playing like Betty White out there." "That's not what your girlfriend says," she quips back, before eating a Snickers and magically transforming back into the player in question. As the white-haired poster girl of the company's "You're Not You When You're Hungry" campaign, Betty shows there's power in being able to laugh at yourself, especially when you have a stunt double.

Betty arrives at the *You Again* premiere at the El Capitan Theatre in Hollywood, California, September 22, 2010.

Shake Things Up

It's easy to get stuck in a routine, so throw something new into the mix every now and then. When we look for different ways to flex our skills, the things we love most can start to feel new again.

NOTHING BREATHES MORE life into a series and excites viewers quite like the introduction of a wild card. That's exactly what Betty brought to the table when she took a role in the final season of the ABC legal drama *The Practice*. As Catherine Piper, Betty plays a scheming senior with a mean streak keen on exacting revenge against her former neighbor, lawyer Alan Shore (James Spader), for the pranks he played on her in his youth. The performance garnered her an Emmy nomination, and following the creation of the show's spin-off, *Boston Legal*, Betty was invited back for another 16 episodes.

Shake Things Up

After taking a job as Alan's secretary, Catherine serves as his personal tormentor-in-chief, where her total lack of filter manages to offend everyone at the firm save for Alan's newest client, a murderer named Bernard Ferrion (Leslie Jordan). The two become friends—that is, until Catherine, fearing he will resume his murderous ways, bludgeons him to death with a skillet. Despite her culpability, she is eventually acquitted for the killing, although she does lose her job. With a newfound taste for breaking the law, Catherine goes on a crime spree: she commits not one but two armed robberies, busts a friend out of a nursing home and (unintentionally) sets fire to her doctor's office after having been prescribed medication that causes her to have a heart attack, all of which she gets away with scot-free. In her final (and somewhat meta) appearance, the octogenarian convinces one of Alan's colleagues to take her lawsuit against ageist broadcast networks that shun programming for older audiences.

By playing a foul-mouthed grandma with a gun, Betty showed a whole new generation of fans she could still push the envelope. Don't be afraid to do the unexpected if it means keeping things fresh.

Betty as Catherine Piper in *Boston Legal*.

Betty and her husband, Allen Ludden, play gin rummy at their home in Westchester, New York, April 29, 1965. A talented singer, the *Password* host released an album titled *Allen Ludden Sings His Favorite Songs* in 1964.

Betty and the love of her life, Allen Ludden, in an undated photo.

Grieve,
Then Keep Living

**Make time to honor your loved ones...and when you're
ready, pick up the pieces and keep moving forward.**

I N EARLY 1980, Betty and Allen Ludden were planning the
construction of their dream house in Carmel, California, when
the couple received terrible news: Allen was diagnosed with
stomach cancer. When it became clear his illness was terminal,
they focused on making the most of their time together. The
following February, the couple journeyed to visit their finished
home. "He slept there two nights," she recalled. Four months later,
Allen passed away at 63. After 18 years of wedded bliss, Betty
suddenly found herself a widow.

Grieve, Then Keep Living

Fortunately, she wasn't alone. Betty's mother, Tess White, then in her 80s, helped guide her through the stages of bereavement. Yet as anyone who's ever lost a loved one knows, part of processing loss involves taking a long, hard look at what you wish you could've done differently. Betty's chief regret: time, or more specifically, the year she spent putting off Allen's proposals. "I wasted a whole year we could have had together," she told Oprah Winfrey in 2015.

Knowing she couldn't allow Allen's passing to cause her to give up on life, Betty poured all of her energy into acting and charity work. A few years later, during her run on *The Golden Girls*, the actress received fan mail from widows seeking her advice on overcoming grief. Moved and honored, she replied to every letter, hoping to help others facing their own battles. She also drew on her loss to play the widow of a missing-in-action World War II pilot in the 2011 Hallmark movie *The Lost Valentine*.

When asked why she never remarried, Betty confessed, "If you had the best, who needs the rest?" There's no formula when it comes to dealing with grief. Take it from Betty: "Replay the good times. Be grateful for the years you had." And keep going.

Jennifer Love Hewitt and Betty White in *The Lost Valentine* (2011).

*"I'm a big cockeyed optimist.
I try to accentuate the positive
as opposed to the negative."*

—BETTY WHITE

Step Out of Your Comfort Zone

You don't have to reinvent yourself to actively pursue ways in which you can round out your talents.

CONSIDERING BETTY'S EXTENSIVE background starring in various successful sitcoms, it can be difficult to remember the entertainment icon as anything more than a comedic actress. Despite her quick comebacks, cheeky remarks and a well-honed talent for improv, Betty's not, in fact, a comedian with a history in stand-up. Rather, she's a bona fide actress who every so often gets to delight audiences by bringing her gravitas to more serious roles.

From 2006 to 2009, Betty played Ann Douglas, the estranged mother of main character Stephanie Forrester (Susan Flannery) on the long-running CBS soap opera *The Bold and the Beautiful*.

Betty White

Betty White
on the set of
*The Bold and
the Beautiful.*

B&B

Betty as Ann Douglas on *The Bold and The Beautiful.*

Step Out of Your Comfort Zone

After decades of refusing to acknowledge the childhood abuse Stephanie suffered at the hands of her overbearing father, Ann experiences a change of heart; at a family Christmas party, she not only apologizes to Stephanie for her complicity but admits she was too frightened of her husband to confront him and put an end to the violence. Just as the two women seem poised to rebuild their relationship, Ann learns she is dying from pancreatic cancer. Eventually, when the end comes, rather than see herself hooked up to machines in a hospital, Ann asks to return to her beloved beach, Paradise Cove, where she peacefully passes away in her daughter's arms, having finally found absolution for her failings as a mother.

It's a mesmerizing spectacle, this dark, sobering character arc drawn out in just under two dozen episodes, and as far a cry from Betty's lighter fare as it gets. Beneath Ann's genteel veneer lurks a monster of a shameful past, and only Betty could pull off her redemption, all because she chose to play it straight. Don't be afraid to test your own limits (creatively speaking) from time to time. What you find might surprise you in the best way possible.

Treat Yourself

Feel free to indulge yourself every now and then. Self-care comes in many forms. It's all about balance.

WHEN IT COMES to longevity, it's easy to think someone like Betty has somehow found a way to bottle the fountain of youth. Sure, it might have something to do with her genes—her parents lived well into their 80s. But Betty's high spirits at such an advanced age can at least partly be attributed to a much more earthly potable: vodka, which she once described to David Letterman as "kind of a hobby." "On the rocks... lots and lots of lemon," she added. "You can't get much better."

Daily helpings of clear liquor aside, the First Lady of Television

Betty White in 2009.

Betty enjoys a Pink's hot dog at the Los Angeles Zoo, June 5, 2008.

Treat Yourself

follows a diet that would make even the most fervent health nut green with envy. "Lunch is usually a hot dog and French fries," she told *Harper's Bazaar* in 2014, "or something equally devilish. Red Whips are my curse." Her hot dog addiction is no joke, either. When the famous Pink's hot dog company in California heard the icon prefers to eat hers sans condiments, they named a plain hot dog in her honor: the "Betty White 'Naked' Dog." She also doesn't deny herself the pleasure of partaking in fried foods. Her recipe for fried chicken wings, for instance, calls for half a cup of butter and one full cup of brown sugar.

When asked about her fitness routine, Betty's answer is simple: "I have a two-story house and a bad memory, so all those trips up and down the stairs take care of my exercise." It's certainly a diet and lifestyle most would be lucky to pull off half as well as she has. Even though the actress has spent most of her life in showbusiness, one thing's abundantly clear: Betty doesn't cut herself short when it comes to indulging in life's simple pleasures. Neither should you.

Betty White as
Elka Ostrovsky in
a 2012 episode of
Hot in Cleveland.

"Retirement is not
in my vocabulary.
They aren't going to get
rid of me that way."

—BETTY WHITE

Betty White and
Mary Steenburgen in
The Proposal (2009).

Love Unconditionally

Accept others as they are, flaws and all.

EVERY COUPLE KNOWS there's a great deal of pressure
that comes with meeting your significant other's family.
This is especially true when you're marrying your so-called
"fiancé" as part of a desperate scheme to obtain a green card like
Sandra Bullock's character, Margaret Tate, in the 2009 romantic
comedy *The Proposal*. If you're lucky, a certain family member
will have your back from the start. That's what Betty White does
as Grandma Annie, the grandmother of the prospective groom,
Andrew Paxton (Ryan Reynolds).

With tensions running high as the couple spends a weekend

Love Unconditionally

with the Paxton family in the remote town of Sitka, Alaska, Annie is a breath of fresh air, doting on Margaret as though she were her own granddaughter. She offers her a quilted blanket, saying, "If you get chilly tonight use this. It has special powers," referring to it as "the baby maker." And if that wasn't enough of a ringing endorsement of her soon-to-be granddaughter-in-law, Annie throws an impromptu bachelorette party and helps fit Margaret in her wedding gown. Later in the film, after Margaret derails the ceremony to confess her less than honorable reasons for wanting to marry Andrew and promptly heads for the airport, Annie goes so far as to fake a (very convincing) heart attack. With the family accompanying her in a medevac helicopter, she pressures the pilot to change course, all so her grandson can catch up with the woman he loves before she can leave for good.

But Annie's selfless spirit is perhaps best summed up when she tells Andrew's father (Craig T. Nelson), "Promise me you'll stand by Andrew even if you don't agree with him," a message we can all take to heart. Show your loved ones how much you care while you can. They might need it more than you know.

Sandra Bullock and
Betty White in
The Proposal (2009).

Betty White as
Vickie Angel in
*Date With the
Angels*, 1957.

It's Your Life

You might not get to choose how everything plays out, but you do have the final say in which paths you take.

THERE'S NO ONE-WAY road to becoming an entertainment legend. It's a sprawling journey filled with bumps and mishaps like unpaid gigs, finding out you didn't nail your audition like you hoped and other setbacks. But with more than 80 years in the business, Betty's seen it all and has still managed to come out on top. Despite her longevity, passion and incredible work ethic, what best sets the icon apart from other ambitious female stars is the simple fact that Betty refused to let other people call the shots when it came to living life on her terms.

It's Your Life

Betty didn't pack up and leave Hollywood when casting agents insisted she was "unphotogenic," nor did she buckle when a role didn't generate as much buzz as she hoped. But in her mid-20s, while working as a voice actress during her marriage to Lane Allen, Betty found herself at a crossroads: She could either stay at home to raise a family, per her husband's wishes, or keep putting herself out there to find her big break in television—on her own. Despite the pressure to give up her career in radio in favor of living the domestic life, Betty dug deep and stayed true to her calling.

"No, I've never regretted it," the legend said about forgoing motherhood to *CBS Sunday Morning* in 2012. Little did Betty know she would go on to win an Emmy Award for playing a housewife just three years after her divorce. As fate would have it, she also got to enjoy motherhood by becoming a stepmother to her husband Allen Ludden's three children. Best of all, she found someone who both recognized her talent and believed in making her dreams a reality, the hallmarks of a marriage based not only on love but mutual respect.

Follow your passions and make the most of every day. Take comfort in knowing that you are the author of your story.

TV RADIO Life

Why Betty White Will Never Be A "Star"

Betty shows off her cover of *TV Radio* magazine in a publicity photo for *Date With the Angels*, 1957.

"I may be a senior,
but so what? I'm still hot."

—BETTY WHITE

Rose (Betty White) and Blanche (Rue McClanahan) cut a rug in a 1989 episode of *The Golden Girls*.

Saturday Night Live cast member Kate McKinnon and Alec Baldwin flirt with Betty onstage at the 70th Emmy Awards in Los Angeles, California, September 17, 2018. As of 2020, Baldwin holds the *SNL* record for most frequent host, while Betty holds the record for being the show's oldest host.

Media Lab Books
For inquiries, call 646-449-8614

Copyright 2021 Topix Media Lab

Published by Topix Media Lab
14 Wall Street, Suite 3C
New York, NY 10005

Printed in China

ISBN-13: 978-1-948174-81-7
ISBN-10: 1-948174-81-2

CEO Tony Romando

Vice President & Publisher Phil Sexton
Senior Vice President of Sales & New Markets Tom Mifsud
Vice President of Retail Sales & Logistics Linda Greenblatt
Director of Finance Vandana Patel
Manufacturing Director Nancy Puskuldjian
Financial Analyst Matthew Quinn
Digital Marketing & Strategy Manager Elyse Gregov

Chief Content Officer Jeff Ashworth
Director of Editorial Operations Courtney Kerrigan
Creative Director Steven Charny
Photo Director Dave Weiss
Executive Editor Tim Baker

Content Editor Juliana Sharaf
Art Director Susan Dazzo
Senior Editor Trevor Courneen
Designer Kelsey Payne
Copy Editor & Fact Checker Tara Sherman

Juliana Sharaf is a writer, editor and *Golden Girls* enthusiast whose past credits include *Everything I Need to Know I Learned from Dolly Parton, John Wayne's Book of American Grit, Smithsonian Ultimate Puzzle Book* and many more. When she isn't penning or planning special projects for Media Lab Books or having craft cocktails on the lanai with family in Florida, she enjoys baking French desserts, mainlining espresso and binge-watching classic films. She and her husband live in New York City.